KING OF
THE NIGHT

A COLLECTION OF
POEMS IN ODE TO THE OWL

By

VARIOUS

WITH AN INTRODUCTORY ESSAY
BY JOHN BURROUGHS

Read & Co.

Copyright © 2021 Ragged Hand

This edition is published by Ragged Hand,
an imprint of Read & Co.

This book is copyright and may not be reproduced or copied in any
way without the express permission of the publisher in writing.

British Library Cataloguing-in-Publication Data
A catalogue record for this book is available
from the British Library.

Read & Co. is part of Read Books Ltd.
For more information visit
www.readandcobooks.co.uk

CONTENTS

3

BIRDS AND POETS

An Essay by John Burroughs

It might almost be said that the birds are all birds of the poets and of no one else, because it is only the poetical temperament that fully responds to them. So true is this, that all the great ornithologists—original namers and biographers of the birds—have been poets in deed if not in word. Audubon is a notable case in point, who, if he had not the tongue or the pen of the poet, certainly had the eye and ear and heart—"the fluid and attaching character"—and the singleness of purpose, the enthusiasm, the unworldliness, the love, that characterize the true and divine race of bards.

So had Wilson, though perhaps not in as large a measure; yet he took fire as only a poet can. While making a journey on foot to Philadelphia, shortly after landing in this country, he caught sight of the red-headed woodpecker flitting among the trees,—a bird that shows like a tricolored scarf among the foliage,—and it so kindled his enthusiasm that his life was devoted to the pursuit of the birds from that day. It was a lucky hit. Wilson had already set up as a poet in Scotland, and was still fermenting when the bird met his eye and suggested to his soul a new outlet for its enthusiasm.

The very idea of a bird is a symbol and a suggestion to the poet. A bird seems to be at the top of the scale, so vehement and intense is his life,—large-brained, large-lunged, hot, ecstatic, his frame charged with buoyancy and his heart with song. The beautiful vagabonds, endowed with every grace, masters of all climes, and knowing no bounds,—how many human aspirations are realized in their free, holiday lives, and how many suggestions to the poet in their flight and song!

Indeed, is not the bird the original type and teacher of the poet, and do we not demand of the human lark or thrush that he "shake out his carols" in the same free and spontaneous manner as his winged prototype? Kingsley has shown how surely the old minnesingers and early ballad-writers have learned of the birds, taking their key-note from the blackbird, or the wood-lark, or the throstle, and giving utterance to a melody as simple and unstudied. Such things as the following were surely caught from the fields or the woods:—

> "She sat down below a thorn,
> Fine flowers in the valley,
> And there has she her sweet babe borne,
> And the green leaves they grow rarely."

Or the best lyric pieces, how like they are to certain bird-songs!—clear, ringing, ecstatic, and suggesting that challenge and triumph which the outpouring of the male bird contains. (Is not the genuine singing, lyrical quality essentially masculine?) Keats and Shelley, perhaps more notably than any other English poets, have the bird organization and the piercing wild-bird cry. This, of course, is not saying that they are the greatest poets, but that they have preëminently the sharp semi-tones of the sparrows and the larks.

But when the general reader thinks of the birds of the poets, he very naturally calls to mind the renowned birds, the lark and the nightingale, Old World melodists, embalmed in Old World poetry, but occasionally appearing on these shores, transported in the verse of some callow singer.

The very oldest poets, the towering antique bards, seem to make little mention of the song-birds. They loved better the soaring, swooping birds of prey, the eagle, the ominous birds, the vultures, the storks and cranes, or the clamorous sea-birds

6

and the screaming hawks. These suited better the rugged, warlike character of the times and the simple, powerful souls of the singers themselves. Homer must have heard the twittering of the swallows, the cry of the plover, the voice of the turtle, and the warble of the nightingale; but they were not adequate symbols to express what he felt or to adorn his theme. Aeschylus saw in the eagle "the dog of Jove," and his verse cuts like a sword with such a conception.

It is not because the old bards were less as poets, but that they were more as men. To strong, susceptible characters, the music of nature is not confined to sweet sounds. The defiant scream of the hawk circling aloft, the wild whinny of the loon, the whooping of the crane, the booming of the bittern, the vulpine bark of the eagle, the loud trumpeting of the migratory geese sounding down out of the midnight sky; or by the seashore, the coast of New Jersey or Long Island, the wild crooning of the flocks of gulls, repeated, continued by the hour, swirling sharp and shrill, rising and falling like the wind in a storm, as they circle above the beach or dip to the dash of the waves,—are much more welcome in certain moods than any and all mere bird-melodies, in keeping as they are with the shaggy and untamed features of ocean and woods, and suggesting something like the Richard Wagner music in the ornithological orchestra.

> "Nor these alone whose notes
> Nice-fingered art must emulate in vain,
> But cawing rooks, and kites that swim sublime
> In still repeated circles, screaming loud,
> The jay, the pie, and even the boding owl,
> That hails the rising moon, have charms for me,"

says Cowper. "I never hear," says Burns in one of his letters, "the loud, solitary whistle of the curlew in a summer noon, or the wild mixing cadence of a troop of gray plovers in an autumnal morning, without feeling an elevation of soul like the enthusiasm of devotion or poetry."

Even the Greek minor poets, the swarm of them that are represented in the Greek Anthology, rarely make affectionate mention of the birds, except perhaps Sappho, whom Ben Jonson makes speak of the nightingale as—

"The dear glad angel of the spring."

The cicada, the locust, and the grasshopper are often referred to, but rarely by name any of the common birds. That Greek grasshopper must have been a wonderful creature. He was a sacred object in Greece, and is spoken of by the poets as a charming songster. What we would say of birds the Greek said of this favorite insect. When Socrates and Phaedrus came to the fountain shaded by the plane-tree, where they had their famous discourse, Socrates said: "Observe the freshness of the spot, how charming and very delightful it is, and how summer-like and shrill it sounds from the choir of grasshoppers." One of the poets in the Anthology finds a grasshopper struggling in a spider's web, which he releases with the words:—

"Go safe and free with your sweet voice of song."

Another one makes the insect say to a rustic who had captured him:—

"Me, the Nymphs' wayside minstrel whose sweet note
O'er sultry hill is heard, and shady grove to float."

Still another sings how a grasshopper took the place of a broken string on his lyre, and "filled the cadence due."

"For while six chords beneath my fingers cried,
He with his tuneful voice the seventh supplied;
The midday songster of the mountain set
His pastoral ditty to my canzonet;
And when he sang, his modulated throat
Accorded with the lifeless string I smote."

While we are trying to introduce the lark in this country, why not try this Pindaric grasshopper also?

It is to the literary poets and to the minstrels of a softer age that we must look for special mention of the song-birds and for poetical rhapsodies upon them. The nightingale is the most general favorite, and nearly all the more noted English poets have sung her praises. To the melancholy poet she is melancholy, and to the cheerful she is cheerful. Shakespeare in one of his sonnets speaks of her song as mournful, while Martial calls her the "most garrulous" of birds. Milton sang:—

"Sweet bird, that shunn'st the noise of folly,
Most musical, most melancholy,
Thee, chantress, oft the woods among
I woo, to hear thy evening song."

To Wordsworth she told another story:—

"O nightingale! thou surely art
A creature of ebullient heart;
These notes of thine,—they pierce and pierce,—
Tumultuous harmony and fierce!
Thou sing'st as if the god of wine
Had helped thee to a valentine;
A song in mockery and despite
Of shades, and dews, and silent night,
And steady bliss, and all the loves
Now sleeping in these peaceful groves."

9

In a like vein Coleridge sang:—

"'T is the merry nightingale
That crowds and hurries and precipitates
With fast, thick warble his delicious notes."

Keats's poem on the nightingale is doubtless more in the spirit of the bird's strain than any other. It is less a description of the song and more the song itself. Hood called the nightingale

"The sweet and plaintive Sappho of the dell."

I mention the nightingale only to point my remarks upon its American rival, the famous mockingbird of the Southern States, which is also a nightingale,—a night-singer,—and which no doubt excels the Old World bird in the variety and compass of its powers. The two birds belong to totally distinct families, there being no American species which answers to the European nightingale, as there are that answer to the robin, the cuckoo, the blackbird, and numerous others. Philomel has the color, manners, and habits of a thrush,—our hermit thrush,—but it is not a thrush at all, but a warbler. I gather from the books that its song is protracted and full rather than melodious,—a capricious, long-continued warble, doubling and redoubling, rising and falling, issuing from the groves and the great gardens, and associated in the minds of the poets with love and moonlight and the privacy of sequestered walks. All our sympathies and attractions are with the bird, and we do not forget that Arabia and Persia are there back of its song.

Our nightingale has mainly the reputation of the caged bird, and is famed mostly for its powers of mimicry, which are truly wonderful, enabling the bird to exactly reproduce and even improve upon the notes of almost any other songster. But in a state of freedom it has a song of its own which is infinitely rich and various. It is a garrulous polyglot when it chooses to be, and there is a dash of the clown and the buffoon in its nature which too often flavors its whole performance, especially in captivity; but in its native haunts, and when its love-passion is upon it, the serious and even grand side of its character comes out.

In Alabama and Florida its song may be heard all through the sultry summer night, at times low and plaintive, then full and strong.

A friend of Thoreau and a careful observer, who has resided in Florida, tells me that this bird is a much more marvelous singer than it has the credit of being. He describes a habit it has of singing on the wing on moonlight nights, that would be worth going South to hear. Starting from a low bush, it mounts in the air and continues its flight apparently to an altitude of several hundred feet, remaining on the wing a number of minutes, and pouring out its song with the utmost clearness and abandon,—a slowly rising musical rocket that fills the night air with harmonious sounds. Here are both the lark and nightingale in one; and if poets were as plentiful down South as they are in New England, we should have heard of this song long ago, and had it celebrated in appropriate verse. But so far only one Southern poet, Wilde, has accredited the bird this song. This he has done in the following admirable sonnet:—

TO THE MOCKINGBIRD

Winged mimic of the woods! thou motley fool!
   Who shall thy gay buffoonery describe?
Thine ever-ready notes of ridicule
   Pursue thy fellows still with jest and gibe.
Wit—sophist—songster—Yorick of thy tribe,
   Thou sportive satirist of Nature's school,
To thee the palm of scoffing we ascribe,
   Arch scoffer, and mad Abbot of Misrule!
For such thou art by day—but all night long
   Thou pour'st a soft, sweet, pensive, solemn strain,

As if thou didst in this, thy moonlight song,
 Like to the melancholy Jaques, complain,
Musing on falsehood, violence, and wrong,
 And sighing for thy motley coat again.

Aside from this sonnet, the mockingbird has got into poetical literature, so far as I know, in only one notable instance, and that in the page of a poet where we would least expect to find him,—a bard who habitually bends his ear only to the musical surge and rhythmus of total nature, and is as little wont to turn aside for any special beauties or points as the most austere of the ancient masters. I refer to Walt Whitman's "Out of the cradle endlessly rocking," in which the mockingbird plays a part. The poet's treatment of the bird is entirely ideal and eminently characteristic. That is to say, it is altogether poetical and not at all ornithological; yet it contains a rendering or free translation of a bird-song—the nocturne of the mockingbird, singing and calling through the night for its lost mate—that I consider quite unmatched in our literature:—

Once, Paumanok,
When the snows had melted, and the Fifth-
month grass was growing,
Up this seashore, in some briers,
Two guests from Alabama—two together,
And their nest, and four light green eggs, spotted with brown,
And every day the he-bird, to and fro, near at hand,
And every day the she-bird, crouched on her nest, silent,
with bright eyes,
And every day I, a curious boy, never too close, never
disturbing them,
Cautiously peering, absorbing, translating.

Shine! Shine! Shine!
Pour down your warmth, great Sun!
While we bask—we two together.

Two together!
Winds blow South, or winds blow North,
Day come white, or night come black,
Home, or rivers and mountains from home,
Singing all time, minding no time,
If we two but keep together.

Till of a sudden,
Maybe killed unknown to her mate,
One forenoon the she-bird crouched not on the nest,
Nor returned that afternoon, nor the next,
Nor ever appeared again.

And thenceforward all summer, in the sound of the sea,
And at night, under the full of the moon, in calmer weather,
Over the hoarse surging of the sea,
Or flitting from brier to brier by day,
I saw, I heard at intervals, the remaining one, the he-bird,
The solitary guest from Alabama.

Blow! blow! blow!
Blow up, sea-winds, along Paumanok's shore!
I wait and I wait, till you blow my mate to me.

Yes, when the stars glistened,
All night long, on the prong of a moss-scalloped stake,
Down, almost amid the slapping waves,
Sat the lone singer, wonderful, causing tears.

He called on his mate:
He poured forth the meanings which I, of all men, know.

Soothe! soothe! soothe!
Close on its wave soothes the wave behind,
And again another behind, embracing and lapping,
every one close,
But my love soothes not me, not me.

Low hangs the moon—it rose late.
Oh it is lagging—oh I think it is heavy with love, with love.

Oh madly the sea pushes, pushes upon the land,
With love—with love.

O night! do I not see my love fluttering
out there among the breakers!
What is that little black thing I see there in the white?

Loud! loud! loud!
Loud I call to you, my love!
High and clear I shoot my voice over the waves:
Surely you must know who is here, is here;
You must know who I am, my love.

Low-hanging moon!
What is that dusky spot in your brown yellow?
Oh it is the shape, the shape of my mate!
O moon, do not keep her from me any longer.

Land! land! O land!
Whichever way I turn, oh I think you could give
my mate back again, if you only would;
For I am almost sure I see her dimly whichever way I look.

O rising stars!
Perhaps the one I want so much will rise, will rise with some
of you.

O throat! O trembling throat!
Sound clearer through the atmosphere!
Pierce the woods, the earth;
Somewhere listening to catch you, must be the one I want.

Shake out, carols!
Solitary here—the night's carols!
Carols of lonesome love! Death's carols!
Carols under that lagging, yellow, waning moon!
Oh, under that moon, where she droops almost down into
the sea!
O reckless, despairing carols.

But soft! sink low! Soft! let me just murmur;
And do you wait a moment, you husky-noised sea;
For somewhere I believe I heard my mate responding to me,
So faint—I must be still, be still to listen!
But not altogether still, for then she might
not come immediately to me.

Hither, my love!
Here I am! Here!
With this just-sustained note I announce myself to you;
This gentle call is for you, my love, for you.

Do not be decoyed elsewhere!
That is the whistle of the wind—it is not my voice;
That is the fluttering, the fluttering of the spray;
Those are the shadows of leaves.

O darkness! Oh in vain!
Oh I am very sick and sorrowful.

The bird that occupies the second place to the nightingale in
British poetical literature is the skylark, a pastoral bird as the

Philomel is an arboreal,—a creature of light and air and motion, the companion of the plowman, the shepherd, the harvester,— whose nest is in the stubble and whose tryst is in the clouds. Its life affords that kind of contrast which the imagination loves,— one moment a plain pedestrian bird, hardly distinguishable from the ground, the next a soaring, untiring songster, reveling in the upper air, challenging the eye to follow him and the ear to separate his notes.

The lark's song is not especially melodious, but is blithesome, sibilant, and unceasing. Its type is the grass, where the bird makes its home, abounding, multitudinous, the notes nearly all alike and all in the same key, but rapid, swarming, prodigal, showering down as thick and fast as drops of rain in a summer shower.

Many noted poets have sung the praises of the lark, or been kindled by his example. Shelley's ode and Wordsworth's "To a Skylark" are well known to all readers of poetry, while every schoolboy will recall Hogg's poem, beginning:—

"Bird of the wilderness,
    Blithesome and cumberless,
Sweet be thy matin o'er moorland and lea!
    Emblem of happiness,
    Blest is thy dwelling-place—
Oh to abide in the desert with thee!"

I heard of an enthusiastic American who went about English fields hunting a lark with Shelley's poem in his hand, thinking no doubt to use it as a kind of guide-book to the intricacies and harmonies of the song.

He reported not having heard any larks, though I have little doubt they were soaring and singing about him all the time, though of course they did not sing to his ear the song that Shelley heard.

The poets are the best natural historians, only you must know

16

how to read them. They translate the facts largely and freely.

A celebrated lady once said to Turner, "I confess I cannot see in nature what you do." "Ah, madam," said the complacent artist, "don't you wish you could!"

Shelley's poem is perhaps better known, and has a higher reputation among literary folk, than Wordsworth's; it is more lyrical and lark-like; but it is needlessly long, though no longer than the lark's song itself, but the lark can't help it, and Shelley can. I quote only a few stanzas:—

> "In the golden lightning
>   Of the sunken sun,
> O'er which clouds are bright'ning
>   Thou dost float and run,
> Like an unbodied joy whose race is just begun.

> "The pale purple even
>   Melts around thy flight;
> Like a star of heaven,
>   In the broad daylight
> Thou art unseen, but yet I hear thy shrill delight,

> "Keen as are the arrows
>   Of that silver sphere,
> Whose intense lamp narrows
>   In the white dawn clear,
> Until we hardly see—we feel that it is there;

> "All the earth and air
>   With thy voice is loud,
> As, when Night is bare,
>   From one lonely cloud
> The moon rains out her beams, and Heaven is overflowed."

Wordsworth has written two poems upon the lark, in one of which he calls the bird "pilgrim of the sky." This is the one quoted by Emerson in "Parnassus." Here is the concluding stanza:—

"Leave to the nightingale her shady wood;
A privacy of glorious light is thine,
Whence thou dost pour upon the world a flood
Of harmony, with instinct more divine;
Type of the wise, who soar, but never roam,
True to the kindred points of heaven and home."

The other poem I give entire:—

"Up with me! up with me into the clouds!
    For thy song, Lark, is strong;
Up with me, up with me into the clouds!
        Singing, singing,
With clouds and sky about thee ringing,
    Lift me, guide me till I find
That spot which seems so to thy mind!

"I have walked through wilderness dreary,
    And to-day my heart is weary;
Had I now the wings of a Faery
    Up to thee would I fly.
There is madness about thee, and joy divine
    In that song of thine;
Lift me, guide me high and high
To thy banqueting-place in the sky.

            "Joyous as morning
Thou art laughing and scorning;
Thou hast a nest for thy love and thy rest,
And, though little troubled with sloth,
Drunken Lark! thou wouldst be loth

To be such a traveler as I.
　　　Happy, happy Liver!
With a soul as strong as a mountain river,
Pouring out praise to the Almighty Giver,
Joy and jollity be with us both!

"Alas! my journey, rugged and uneven,
Through prickly moors or dusty ways must wind;
But hearing thee, or others of thy kind,
As full of gladness and as free of heaven,
I, with my fate contented, will plod on,
And hope for higher raptures, when life's day is done."

But better than either—better and more than a hundred pages—is Shakespeare's simple line,—

"Hark, hark, the lark at heaven's gate sings,"

or John Lyly's, his contemporary,—

　　　"Who is't now we hear?
None but the lark so shrill and clear;
Now at heaven's gate she claps her wings,
The morn not waking till she sings."

We have no well-known pastoral bird in the Eastern States that answers to the skylark. The American pipit or titlark and the shore lark, both birds of the far north, and seen in the States only in fall and winter, are said to sing on the wing in a similar strain. Common enough in our woods are two birds that have many of the habits and manners of the lark—the water-thrush and the golden-crowned thrush, or oven-bird. They are both walkers, and the latter frequently sings on the wing up aloft after the manner of the lark. Starting from its low perch, it rises in a spiral flight far above the tallest trees, and breaks out in a clear, ringing, ecstatic song, sweeter and more richly modulated than the skylark's, but brief, ceasing almost before you have noticed it; whereas the skylark goes singing away after you have forgotten him and returned to him half a dozen times.

But on the Great Plains, of the West there; is a bird whose song resembles the skylark's quite closely and is said to be not at all inferior. This is Sprague's pipit, sometimes called the Missouri skylark, an excelsior songster, which from far up in the transparent blue rains down its notes for many minutes together. It is, no doubt, destined to figure in the future poetical literature of the West.

Throughout the northern and eastern parts of the Union the lark would find a dangerous rival in the bobolink, a bird that has no European prototype, and no near relatives anywhere, standing quite alone, unique, and, in the qualities of hilarity and musical tintinnabulation, with a song unequaled. He has already a secure place in general literature, having been laureated by no less a poet than Bryant, and invested with a lasting human charm in the sunny page of Irving, and is the only one of our songsters, I believe, that the mockingbird cannot parody or imitate. He affords the most marked example of exuberant pride, and a glad, rollicking, holiday spirit, that can be seen among our birds. Every note expresses complacency and glee. He is a beau of the first pattern, and, unlike any other bird of my acquaintance, pushes his gallantry to the point of wheeling gayly into the train of every female that comes along, even after the season of courtship is over and the matches are all settled; and when she leads him on too wild a chase, he turns, lightly about and breaks out with a song is precisely analogous to a burst of gay and self-satisfied laughter, as much as to say, *"Ha! ha! ha! I must have my fun, Miss Silverthimble, thimble, thimble, if I break every heart in the meadow, see, see, see!"*

At the approach of the breeding season the bobolink undergoes a complete change; his form changes, his color changes, his flight changes. From mottled brown or brindle he becomes black and white, earning, in some localities, the shocking name of "skunk bird;" his small, compact form becomes broad and conspicuous, and his ordinary flight is laid aside for a mincing, affected gait, in which he seems to use only the very tips of his wings. It is very noticeable what a contrast he presents to his mate at this season, not only in color but in manners, she being as shy and retiring as he is forward and hilarious. Indeed, she seems disagreeably serious and indisposed to any fun or jollity, scurrying away at his approach, and apparently annoyed at every endearing word and look. It is surprising that all this parade of plumage and tinkling of cymbals should be gone through with and persisted in to please a creature so coldly indifferent as she really seems to be. If Robert O'Lincoln has been stimulated into acquiring this holiday uniform and this musical gift by the approbation of Mrs. Robert, as Darwin, with his sexual selection principle, would have us believe, then there must have been a time when the females of this tribe were not quite so chary of their favors as they are now. Indeed, I never knew a female bird of any kind that did not appear utterly indifferent to the charms of voice and plumage that the male birds are so fond of displaying. But I am inclined to believe that the males think only of themselves and of outshining each other, and not at all of the approbation of their mates, as, in an analogous case in a higher species, it is well known whom the females dress for, and whom they want to kill with envy!

I know of no other song-bird that expresses so much self-consciousness and vanity, and comes so near being an ornithological coxcomb. The red-bird, the yellowbird, the indigo-bird, the oriole, the cardinal grosbeak, and others, all birds of brilliant plumage and musical ability, seem quite unconscious of self, and neither by tone nor act challenge the admiration of the beholder.

By the time the bobolink reaches the Potomac, in September, he has degenerated into a game-bird that is slaughtered by tens of thousands in the marshes. I think the prospects now are of his gradual extermination, as gunners and sportsmen are clearly on the increase, while the limit of the bird's productivity in the North has no doubt been reached long ago. There are no more meadows to be added to his domain there, while he is being waylaid and cut off more and more on his return to the South. It is gourmand eat gourmand, until in half a century more I expect the blithest and merriest of our meadow songsters will have disappeared before the rapacity of human throats.

But the poets have had a shot at him in good time, and have preserved some of his traits. Bryant's poem on this subject does not compare with his lines "To a Water-Fowl,"—a subject so well suited to the peculiar, simple, and deliberate motion of his mind; at the same time it is fit that the poet who sings of "The Planting of the Apple-Tree" should render into words the song of "Robert of Lincoln." I subjoin a few stanzas:—

ROBERT OF LINCOLN

Merrily swinging on brier and weed,
    Near to the nest of his little dame,
Over the mountain-side or mead,
    Robert of Lincoln is telling his name:
        Bob-o'-link, bob-o'-link,
        Spink, spank, spink:
Snug and safe is that nest of ours,
Hidden among the summer flowers.
        Chee, chee, chee.

Robert of Lincoln is gayly drest,
    Wearing a bright black wedding-coat,
White are his shoulders and white his crest,
    Hear him call in his merry note:
        Bob-o'-link, bob-o'-link,
        Spink, spank, spink:

Look what a nice new coat is mine,
Sure there was never a bird so fine.
　　Chee, chee, chee.

Robert of Lincoln's Quaker wife,
　Pretty and quiet, with plain brown wings,
Passing at home a patient life,
　Broods in the grass while her husband sings.
　　Bob-o'-link, bob-o'-link,
　　Spink, spank, spink:
Brood, kind creature; you need not fear
Thieves and robbers while I am here.
　　Chee, chee, chee.

But it has been reserved for a practical ornithologist, Mr. Wilson Flagg, to write by far the best poem on the bobolink that I have yet seen. It is much more in the mood and spirit of the actual song than Bryant's poem:—

THE O'LINCOLN FAMILY

A flock of merry singing-birds were sporting in the grove;
Some were warbling cheerily, and some were making love:
There were Bobolincon, Wadolincon,
Winterseeble, Conquedle,—
A livelier set was never led by tabor, pipe, or fiddle,—
Crying, "Phew, shew, Wadolincon, see, see, Bobolincon,
Down among the tickletops, hiding in the buttercups!
I know the saucy chap, I see his shining cap
Bobbing in the clover there—see, see, see!"

Up flies Bobolincon, perching on an apple-tree,
Startled by his rival's song, quickened by his raillery.
Soon he spies the rogue afloat, curveting in the air,
And merrily he turns about, and warns him to beware!
"'T is you that would a-wooing go, down among the rushes O!
But wait a week, till flowers are cheery,—
wait a week,and, ere you marry,
Be sure of a house wherein to tarry!
Wadolink, Whiskodink, Tom Denny, wait, wait, wait!"

Every one's a funny fellow; every one's a little mellow;
Follow, follow, follow, follow, o'er the hill and in the hollow!
Merrily, merrily, there they hie; now they rise and now they fly;
They cross and turn, and in and out, and down
in the middle, and wheel about,—
With a "Phew, shew, Wadolincon! listen to me, Bobolincon!—
Happy's the wooing that's speedily doing, that's speedily doing,
That's merry and over with the bloom of the clover!
Bobolincon, Wadolincon, Winterseeble, follow, follow me!"

Many persons, I presume, have admired Wordsworth's poem
on the cuckoo, without recognizing its truthfulness, or how
thoroughly, in the main, the description applies to our own

species. If the poem had been written in New England or New York, it could not have suited our case better:—

"O blithe New-comer! I have heard,
 I hear thee and rejoice,
O Cuckoo! shall I call thee Bird,
 Or but a wandering Voice?

"While I am lying on the grass,
 Thy twofold shout I hear,
From hill to hill it seems to pass,
 At once far off, and near.

"Though babbling only to the Vale,
 Of sunshine and of flowers,
Thou bringest unto me a tale
 Of visionary hours.

"Thrice welcome, darling of the Spring!
 Even yet thou art to me
No bird, but an invisible thing,
 A voice, a mystery;

"The same whom in my schoolboy days
 I listened to; that Cry
Which made me look a thousand ways
 In bush, and tree, and sky.

"To seek thee did I often rove
 Through woods and on the green;
And thou wert still a hope, a love;
 Still longed for, never seen.

"And I can listen to thee yet;
　Can lie upon the plain
And listen, till I do beget
　That golden time again.

"O blesséd Bird! the earth we pace
　Again appears to be
An unsubstantial, faery place;
　That is fit home for thee!"

Logan's stanzas, "To the Cuckoo," have less merit both as poetry and natural history, but they are older, and doubtless the latter poet benefited by them. Burke admired them so much that, while on a visit to Edinburgh, he sought the author out to compliment him:—

"Hail, beauteous stranger of the grove!
　Thou messenger of spring!
Now Heaven repairs thy rural seat,
　And woods thy welcome sing.

"What time the daisy decks the green,
　Thy certain voice we hear;
Hast thou a star to guide thy path,
　Or mark the rolling year?

* * * * *

"The schoolboy, wandering through the wood
　To pull the primrose gay,
Starts, the new voice of spring to hear,
　And imitates thy lay.

* * * * *

"Sweet bird! thy bower is ever green,
   Thy sky is ever clear;
Thou hast no sorrow in thy song,
   No winter in thy year."

The European cuckoo is evidently a much gayer bird than ours, and much more noticeable.

"Hark, how the jolly cuckoos sing
'Cuckoo!' to welcome in the spring,"

says John Lyly three hundred years agone. Its note is easily imitated, and boys will render it so perfectly as to deceive any but the shrewdest ear. An English lady tells me its voice reminds one of children at play, and is full of gayety and happiness. It is a persistent songster, and keeps up its call from morning to night. Indeed, certain parts of Wordsworth's poem—those that refer to the bird as a mystery, a wandering, solitary voice—seem to fit our bird better than the European species. Our cuckoo is in fact a solitary wanderer, repeating its loud, guttural call in the depths of the forest, and well calculated to arrest the attention of a poet like Wordsworth, who was himself a kind of cuckoo, a solitary voice, syllabling the loneliness that broods over streams and woods,—

"And once far off, and near."

Our cuckoo is not a spring bird, being seldom seen or heard in the North before late in May. He is a great devourer of canker-worms, and, when these pests appear, he comes out of his forest seclusion and makes excursions through the orchards stealthily and quietly, regaling himself upon those pulpy, fuzzy titbits. His coat of deep cinnamon brown has a silky gloss and is very beautiful. His note or call is not musical but loud, and has in a remarkable degree the quality of remoteness and introvertedness.

It is like a vocal legend, and to the farmer bodes rain.

It is worthy of note, and illustrates some things said farther back, that birds not strictly denominated songsters, but criers like the cuckoo, have been quite as great favorites with the poets, and have received as affectionate treatment at their hands, as have the song-birds. One readily recalls Emerson's "Titmouse," Trowbridge's "Pewee," Celia Thaxter's "Sandpiper," and others of a like character.

It is also worthy of note that the owl appears to be a greater favorite with the poets than the proud, soaring hawk. The owl is doubtless the more human and picturesque bird; then he belongs to the night and its weird effects. Bird of the silent wing and expansive eye, grimalkin in feathers, feline, mousing, haunting ruins" and towers, and mocking the midnight stillness with thy uncanny cry! The owl is the great bugaboo of the feathered tribes. His appearance by day is hailed by shouts of alarm and derision from nearly every bird that flies, from crows down to sparrows. They swarm about him like flies, and literally mob him back into his dusky retreat. Silence is as the breath of his nostrils to him, and the uproar that greets him when he emerges into the open day seems to alarm and confuse him as it does the pickpocket when everybody cries Thief.

But the poets, I say, have not despised him:—

> "The lark is but a bumpkin fowl;
>   He sleeps in his nest till morn;
> But my blessing upon the jolly owl
>   That all night blows his horn."

Both Shakespeare and Tennyson have made songs about him. This is Shakespeare's, from "Love's Labor's Lost," and perhaps has reference to the white or snowy owl:—

"When icicles hang by the wall,
　And Dick the shepherd blows his nail,
And Tom bears logs into the hall,
　And milk comes frozen home in pail;
When blood is nipped and ways be foul,
Then nightly sings the staring owl,
　　Tu-whoo!
Tu-whit! tu-whoo! a merry note,
While greasy Joan doth keel the pot.

"When all aloud the wind doth blow,
　And coughing drowns the parson's saw,
And birds sit brooding in the snow,
　And Marian's nose looks red and raw;
When roasted crabs hiss in the bowl,
Then nightly sings the staring owl,
　　Tu-whoo!
Tu-whit! Tu-whoo! a merry note,
While greasy Joan doth keel the pot."

There is, perhaps, a slight reminiscence of this song in Tennyson's "Owl:"—

"When cats run home and light is come,
　And dew is cold upon the ground,
And the far-off stream is dumb,
　And the whirring sail goes round,
　And the whirring sail goes round;
　　Alone and warming his five wits,
　　The white owl in the belfry sits.

"When merry milkmaids click the latch,
  And rarely smells the new-mown hay,
And the cock hath sung beneath the thatch
    Twice or thrice his roundelay,
    Twice or thrice his roundelay;
      Alone and warming his five wits,
      The white owl in the belfry sits."

Tennyson has not directly celebrated any of the more famous birds, but his poems contain frequent allusions to them. The

"Wild bird, whose warble, liquid sweet,
  Rings Eden through the budded quicks,
  Oh, tell me where the senses mix,
  Oh, tell me where the passions meet,"

of "In Memoriam," is doubtless the nightingale. And here we have the lark:—

"Now sings the woodland loud and long,
  And distance takes a lovelier hue,
  And drowned in yonder living blue
The lark becomes a sightless song."

And again in this from "A Dream of Fair Women:"—

"Then I heard
A noise of some one coming through the lawn,
  And singing clearer than the crested bird
    That claps his wings at dawn."

The swallow is a favorite bird with Tennyson, and is frequently mentioned, beside being the principal figure in one of those charming love-songs in "The Princess."

His allusions to the birds, as to any other natural feature, show him to be a careful observer, as when he speaks of

"The swamp, where hums the dropping snipe."

His single bird-poem, aside from the song I have quoted, is "The Blackbird," the Old World prototype of our robin, as if our bird had doffed the aristocratic black for a more democratic suit on reaching these shores. In curious contrast to the color of its plumage is its beak, which is as yellow as a kernel of Indian corn. The following are the two middle stanzas of the poem:—

"Yet, though I spared thee all the spring,
    Thy sole delight is, sitting still,
    With that gold dagger of thy bill
To fret the summer jenneting.

"A golden bill! the silver tongue
    Cold February loved is dry;
    Plenty corrupts the melody
That made thee famous once, when young."

Shakespeare, in one of his songs, alludes to the blackbird as the ouzel-cock; indeed, he puts quite a flock of birds in this song:—

"The ouzel-cock so black of hue,
    With orange tawny bill;
The throstle with his note so true,
    The wren with little quill;
The finch, the sparrow, and the lark,
    The plain song cuckoo gray,
Whose note full many a man doth mark,
    And dares not answer nay."

So far as external appearances are concerned,—form, plumage, grace of manner,—no one ever had a less promising subject than had Trowbridge in the "Pewee." This bird, if not the plainest dressed, is the most unshapely in the woods. It is stiff and abrupt in its manners and sedentary in its habits, sitting around all day, in the dark recesses of the woods, on the dry twigs and branches, uttering now and then its plaintive cry, and "with many a flirt and flutter" snapping up its insect game.

The pewee belongs to quite a large family of birds, all of whom have strong family traits, and who are not the most peaceable and harmonious of the sylvan folk. They are pugnacious, harsh-voiced, angular in form and movement, with flexible tails and broad, flat, bristling beaks that stand to the face at the angle of a turn-up nose, and most of them wear a black cap pulled well down over their eyes. Their heads are large, neck and legs short, and elbows sharp. The wild Irishman of them all is the great crested flycatcher, a large, leather-colored or sandy-complexioned bird that prowls through the woods, uttering its harsh, uncanny note and waging fierce warfare upon its fellows. The exquisite of the family, and the braggart of the orchard, is the kingbird, a bully that loves to strip the feathers off its more timid neighbors such as the bluebird, that feeds on the stingless bees of the hive, the drones, and earns the reputation of great boldness by teasing large hawks, while it gives a wide berth to little ones.

The best beloved of them all is the phoebe-bird, one of the firstlings of the spring, of whom so many of our poets have made affectionate mention.

The wood pewee is the sweetest voiced, and, notwithstanding the ungracious things I have said of it and of its relations, merits to the full all Trowbridge's pleasant fancies. His poem is indeed a very careful study of the bird and its haunts, and is good poetry as well as good ornithology:—

"The listening Dryads hushed the woods;
   The boughs were thick, and thin and few
   The golden ribbons fluttering through;
Their sun-embroidered, leafy hoods
   The lindens lifted to the blue;
Only a little forest-brook
The farthest hem of silence shook;
When in the hollow shades I heard—
Was it a spirit or a bird?
Or, strayed from Eden, desolate,
Some Peri calling to her mate,
Whom nevermore her mate would cheer?
   'Pe-ri! pe-ri! peer!'

* * * * *

"To trace it in its green retreat
   I sought among the boughs in vain;
   And followed still the wandering strain,
So melancholy and so sweet,
   The dim-eyed violets yearned with pain.
'T was now a sorrow in the air,
Some nymph's immortalized despair
Haunting the woods and waterfalls;
And now, at long, sad intervals,
Sitting unseen in dusky shade,
His plaintive pipe some fairy played,
With long-drawn cadence thin and clear,—
   'Pe-wee! pe-wee! peer!'

"Long-drawn and clear its closes were—
  As if the hand of Music through
  The sombre robe of Silence drew
A thread of golden gossamer;
  So pure a flute the fairy blew.
Like beggared princes of the wood,
In silver rags the birches stood;
The hemlocks, lordly counselors,
Were dumb; the sturdy servitors,
In beechen jackets patched and gray,
Seemed waiting spellbound all the day
That low, entrancing note to hear,—
  'Pe-wee! pe-wee! peer!'

"I quit the search, and sat me down
  Beside the brook, irresolute,
  And watched a little bird in suit
Of sober olive, soft and brown,
  Perched in the maple branches, mute;
With greenish gold its vest was fringed,
Its tiny cap was ebon-tinged,
With ivory pale its wings were barred,
And its dark eyes were tender-starred.
"Dear bird," I said, "what is thy name?"
And thrice the mournful answer came,
So faint and far, and yet so near,—
  'Pe-wee! pe-wee! peer!'

"For so I found my forest bird,—
　The pewee of the loneliest woods,
　Sole singer in these solitudes,
Which never robin's whistle stirred,
　Where never bluebird's plume intrudes.
Quick darting through the dewy morn,
The redstart trilled his twittering horn
And vanished in thick boughs; at even,
Like liquid pearls fresh showered from heaven,
The high notes of the lone wood thrush
Fell on the forest's holy hush;
But thou all day complainest here,—
　'Pe-wee! pe-wee! peer!'"

Emerson's best natural history poem is the "Humble-Bee,"—a poem as good in its way as Burns's poem on the mouse; but his later poem, "The Titmouse," has many of the same qualities, and cannot fail to be acceptable to both poet and naturalist.

The chickadee is indeed a truly Emersonian bird, and the poet shows him to be both a hero and a philosopher. Hardy, active, social, a winter bird no less than a summer, a defier of both frost and heat, lover of the pine-tree, and diligent searcher after truth in the shape of eggs and larvae of insects, preëminently a New England bird, clad in black and ashen gray, with a note the most cheering and reassuring to be heard in our January woods,—I know of none other of our birds so well calculated to captivate the Emersonian muse.

Emerson himself is a northern hyperborean genius,—a winter bird with a clear, saucy, cheery call, and not a passionate summer songster. His lines have little melody to the ear, but they have the vigor and distinctness of all pure and compact things. They are like the needles of the pine—"the snow loving pine"— more than the emotional foliage of the deciduous trees, and the titmouse becomes them well:—

"Up and away for life! be fleet!—
The frost-king ties my fumbling feet,
Sings in my ears, my hands are stones,
Curdles the blood to the marble bones,
Tugs at the heart-strings, numbs the sense,
And hems in life with narrowing fence.
Well, in this broad bed lie and sleep,—
The punctual stars will vigil keep,—
Embalmed by purifying cold;
The wind shall sing their dead march old,
The snow is no ignoble shroud,
The moon thy mourner, and the cloud.

"Softly,—but this way fate was pointing,
'T was coming fast to such anointing,
When piped a tiny voice hard by,
Gay and polite, a cheerful cry,
Chick-chickadeedee! saucy note,
Out of sound heart and merry throat,
As if it said 'Good day, good sir!
Fine afternoon, old passenger!
Happy to meet you in these places,
Where January brings few faces.'

"This poet, though he lived apart,
Moved by his hospitable heart,
Sped, when I passed his sylvan fort,
To do the honors of his court,
As fits a feathered lord of land;
Flew near, with soft wing grazed my hands
Hopped on the bough, then darting low,
Prints his small impress on the snow,
Shows feats of his gymnastic play,
Head downward, clinging to the spray.

"Here was this atom in full breath,
Hurling defiance at vast death;
This scrap of valor just for play
Fronts the north-wind in waistcoat gray,
As if to shame my weak behavior;
I greeted loud my little savior,
'You pet! what dost here? and what for?
In these woods, thy small Labrador,
At this pinch, wee San Salvador!
What fire burns in that little chest,
So frolic, stout, and self-possest?
Henceforth I wear no stripe but thine;
Ashes and jet all hues outshine.
Why are not diamonds black and gray,
To ape thy dare-devil array?
And I affirm, the spacious North
Exists to draw thy virtue forth.
I think no virtue goes with size;
The reason of all cowardice
Is, that men are overgrown,
And, to be valiant, must come down
To the titmouse dimension.'

* * * * *

"I think old Caesar must have heard
In northern Gaul my dauntless bird,
And, echoed in some frosty wold,
Borrowed thy battle-numbers bold.
And I will write our annals new
And thank thee for a better clew.
I, who dreamed not when I came here
To find the antidote of fear,
Now hear thee say in Roman key,
Poean! Veni, vidi, vici."

A late bird-poem, and a good one of its kind, is Celia Thaxter's "Sandpiper," which recalls Bryant's "Water-Fowl" in its successful rendering of the spirit and atmosphere of the scene, and the distinctness with which the lone bird, flitting along the beach, is brought before the mind. It is a woman's or a feminine poem, as Bryant's is characteristically a man's.

The sentiment or feeling awakened by any of the aquatic fowls is preëminently one of loneliness. The wood duck which your approach starts from the pond or the marsh, the loon neighing down out of the April sky, the wild goose, the curlew, the stork, the bittern, the sandpiper, awaken quite a different train of emotions from those awakened by the land-birds. They all have clinging to them some reminiscence and suggestion of the sea. Their cries echo its wildness and desolation; their wings are the shape of its billows.

Of the sandpipers there are many varieties, found upon the coast and penetrating inland along the rivers and water-courses, one of the most interesting of the family, commonly called the "tip-up," going up all the mountain brooks and breeding in the sand along their banks; but the characteristics are the same in all, and the eye detects little difference except in size.

The walker on the beach sees it running or flitting before him, following up the breakers and picking up the aquatic insects left on the sands; and the trout-fisher along the farthest inland stream likewise intrudes upon its privacy. Flitting along from stone to stone seeking its food, the hind part of its body "teetering" up and down, its soft gray color blending it with the pebbles and the rocks, or else skimming up or down the stream on its long, convex wings, uttering its shrill cry, the sandpiper is not a bird of the sea merely; and Mrs. Thaxter's poem is as much for the dweller inland as for the dweller upon the coast:—

THE SANDPIPER

Across the narrow beach we flit,
  One little sandpiper and I;
And fast I gather, bit by bit,
  The scattered driftwood bleached and dry.
The wild waves reach their hands for it,
  The wild wind raves, the tide runs high,
As up and down the beach we flit,—
  One little sandpiper and I.

Above our heads the sullen clouds
  Scud black and swift across the sky;
Like silent ghosts in misty shrouds
  Stand out the white lighthouses high.
Almost as far as eye can reach
  I see the close-reefed vessels fly,
As fast we flit along the beach,—
  One little sandpiper and I.

I watch him as he skims along,
  Uttering his sweet and mournful cry;
He starts not at my fitful song,
  Or flash of fluttering drapery;
He has no thought of any wrong;
  He scans me with a fearless eye.
Stanch friends are we, well tried and strong,
  The little sandpiper and I.

Comrade, where wilt thou be to-night
  When the loosed storm breaks furiously?
My driftwood fire will burn so bright!
  To what warm shelter canst thou fly?
I do not fear for thee, though wroth
  The tempest rushes through the sky;

For are we not God's children both,
Thou, little sandpiper, and I?

Others of our birds have been game for the poetic muse, but in most cases the poets have had some moral or pretty conceit to convey, and have not loved the bird first. Mr. Lathrop preaches a little in his pleasant poem, "The Sparrow," but he must some time have looked upon the bird with genuine emotion to have written the first two stanzas:—

"Glimmers gay the leafless thicket
    Close beside my garden gate,
Where, so light, from post to wicket,
    Hops the sparrow, blithe, sedate:
        Who, with meekly folded wing,
        Comes to sun himself and sing.

"It was there, perhaps, last year,
    That his little house he built;
For he seems to perk and peer,
    And to twitter, too, and tilt
        The bare branches in between,
        With a fond, familiar mien."

The bluebird has not been overlooked, and Halleek, Longfellow, and Mrs. Sigourney have written poems upon him, but from none of them does there fall that first note of his in early spring,—a note that may be called the violet of sound, and as welcome to the ear, heard above the cold, damp earth; as is its floral type to the eye a few weeks later Lowell's two lines come nearer the mark:—

"The bluebird, shifting his light load of song
From post to post along the cheerless fence."

40

Or the first swallow that comes twittering up the southern valley, laughing a gleeful, childish laugh, and awakening such memories in the heart, who has put him in a poem? So the hummingbird, too, escapes through the finest meshes of rhyme.

The most melodious of our songsters, the wood thrush and the hermit thrush,—birds whose strains, more than any others, express harmony and serenity,—have not yet, that I am aware, had reared to them their merited poetic monument, unless, indeed, Whitman has done this service for the hermit thrush in his "President Lincoln's Burial Hymn." Here the threnody is blent of three chords, the blossoming lilac, the evening star, and the hermit thrush, the latter playing the most prominent part throughout the composition. It is the exalting and spiritual utterance of the "solitary singer" that calms and consoles the poet when the powerful shock of the President's assassination comes upon him, and he flees from the stifling atmosphere and offensive lights and conversation of the house,—

"Forth to hiding, receiving night that talks not,
Down to the shores of the water, the path by the swamp in the dimness,
To the solemn shadowy cedars and ghostly pines so still."

Numerous others of our birds would seem to challenge attention by their calls and notes. There is the Maryland yellowthroat, for instance, standing in the door of his bushy tent, and calling out as you approach, *"which way, sir! which way, sir!"* If he says this to the ear of common folk, what would he not say to the poet? One of the peewees says *"stay there!"* with great emphasis. The cardinal grosbeak calls out *"what cheer"* *"what cheer;"* " the bluebird says *"purity,"* *"purity,"* *"purity;"* the brown thrasher, or ferruginous thrush, according to Thoreau, calls out to the farmer planting his corn, *"drop it,"* *"drop it," "cover it up," "cover it up"* The yellow-breasted chat says *"who,"* *"who"* and *"tea-boy"* What the robin says, caroling that simple strain from the top of the tall maple, or the crow with his hardy haw-haw, or the pedestrain meadowlark sounding his piercing and long-drawn note in the spring meadows, the poets ought to be able to tell us. I only know the birds all have a language which is very expressive, and which is easily translatable into the human tongue.

AN ESSAY FROM
Birds and Poets, 1877

THE WESTERN HORNED OWL

By William Kerr Higley

Bubo virginianus subarcticus.

Among the birds of prey (Raptores) none are better known, more written about or more cosmopolitan than that nocturnal division (Family Strigidae), which includes the two hundred or more species of Owls. From the Arctic regions of the north to the Antarctic regions of the south they are known. Most of the genera are represented in both hemispheres, though eight are peculiar to the Old World and three to the New. The majority of the species finds a home in the forests, though a few live in marshes and on the plains. Some invade the buildings of civilization and may be found in the unfrequented towers of churches and in outbuildings.

Disliked by all birds its appearance during the day is the signal for a storm of protests and, knowing that there is little need of fear of his power at this time, they flock about him, pecking and teasing him till he is obliged to retreat to his obscure roosting place.

The Owls in most countries of both the New World as well as the Old are regarded as birds of ill omen and messengers of woe, and are protected from harm by some uncivilized and superstitious peoples, some believing that spirits of the wicked reside in their bodies. By others they have been called "Devil's Birds." The belief of some unlearned people in the close relationship of the Owl with death and the grave dates back at least to the time of Shakespeare, who speaks of the Owl's hoot as "A song of death." Among the ancient races only the Athenians seem not to have possessed this popular fear and superstition. They venerated the Owl and regarded it as the favourite bird of Minerva. On the other hand the Romans looked upon the Owl with fear and detestation, dreading its appearance as the embodiment of all evil and the omen of unfortunate events to come. By them the Owl was consecrated to Proserpine, the wife of Hades and queen of the underworld. Pliny tells us that the city of Rome underwent a solemn cleansing because of the visit of one of these birds. When the unearthly character of their cries and their quiet, spirit-like motion, as they fly through the night hours, are taken into, consideration, it is not surprising that they have been and are held in awe and dread by many people. The characteristics of the two sexes are practically the same, except that the female is somewhat the larger. The young resemble the adults, but are usually darker in colour.

Excepting those species that are whitish in colour, the Owls are usually a mixture of black, brown, rufous gray, yellow and white, and barring is common on the wings and tail. Their bills are blackish, dusky or yellowish. Their eyes are so fixed that they have little power of turning the eye-balls and thus are obliged to turn the head when they wish to change their range of vision. This they do with great rapidity, in fact, the motion is so rapid that without close observation the bird seems to turn its head in one direction for several revolutions if the object looked at passes around the perch upon which the Owl rests. A remarkable characteristic is the reversible fourth toe or digit, enabling the Owl to perch with either one or two toes behind.

Mr. Evans tells us that "the note varies from a loud hoot to a low, muffled sound or a clear, musical cry; the utterance of both young and adults being in some cases a cat-like mew, while the screech-owl snores when stationary. The hoot is said to be produced by closing the bill, puffing out the throat, and then liberating the air, a proceeding comparable to that of the

Bitterns. On the whole the voice is mournful and monotonous, but occasionally it resembles a shrill laugh." The utterances of the Owls are, however, quite various. Some species will give a piercing scream and hiss like an angry cat when disturbed. . .

. . .The Owl has long been an inspiration to the poets, due to its odd appearance and uncanny actions during the daylight hours, the wise expression of its face, and its quiet flight during the weird hours of the night.

"The lark is but a bumpkin fowl;
He sleeps in liis nest till morn;
But my blessing upon the jolly owl
That all night blows his horn."

AN EXCERPT FROM
Birds and Nature, Vol VIII, N.o. 5,
December 1900

KING OF THE NIGHT

A COLLECTION OF
POEMS IN ODE TO THE OWL

THE SEASONS

WHEN ICICLES HANG BY THE WALL

By William Shakespeare

When icicles hang by the wall
    And Dick the shepherd blows his nail
And Tom bears logs into the hall
    And milk comes frozen home in pail,
When blood is nipp'd and ways be foul,
Then nightly sings the staring owl,
        Tu-whit;
Tu-who, a merry note,
While greasy Joan doth keel the pot.

When all aloud the wind doth blow
    And coughing drowns the parson's saw
And birds sit brooding in the snow
    And Marian's nose looks red and raw,
When roasted crabs hiss in the bowl,
Then nightly sings the staring owl,
        Tu-whit;
Tu-who, a merry note,
While greasy Joan doth keel the pot.

SWEET SUFFOLK OWL

By Thomas Vautor

Sweet Suffolk owl, so trimly dight
With feathers, like a lady bright;
Thou sing'st alone, sitting by night,
  "Te whit! Te whoo!"

Thy note that forth so freely rolls
With shrill command the mouse controls;
And sings a dirge for dying souls.
  "Te whit! Te whoo!

THE TWO OWLS
AND THE SPARROW

By John Gay

TWO formal Owls together sate,
Conferring thus in solemn chat.
How is the modern taste decay'd!
Where's the respect to wisdom paid?
Our worth the Grecian sages knew,
They gave our sires the honour due,
They weigh'd the dignity of fowls,
And pry'd into the depth of owls.
Athens, the seat of learned fame,
With gen'ral voice rever'd our name;
On merit title was conferr'd,
And all ador'd th' Athenian bird.

   Brother, you reason well, replies
The solemn mate, with half-shut eyes;
Right. Athens was the seat of learning,
And truly wisdom is discerning.
Besides, on Pallas' helm we sit,
The type and ornament of wit:
But now, alas, we're quite neglected,
And a pert sparrow's more respected.

   A Sparrow, who was lodg'd beside,
O'erhears them sooth each other's pride,
And thus he nimbly vents his heat.

   Who meets a fool must find conceit.
I grant, you were at Athens grac'd,

And on Minerva's helm were plac'd,
But ev'ry bird that wings the sky,
Except an owl, can tell you why.
From hence they taught their schools to know
How false we judge by outward show,
That we should never looks esteem,
Since fools as wise as you might seem.
Would ye contempt and scorn avoid,
Let your vain-glory be destroy'd;
Humble your arrogance of thought,
Pursue the ways by nature taught,
So shall ye find delicious fare,
And grateful farmers praise your care,
So shall sleek mice your chase reward,
And no keen cat find more regard.

THE OWL
AND THE FARMER

By John Gay

An Owl of grave deport and mien,
Who (like the Turk) was seldom seen,
Within a barn had chose his station,
As fit for prey and contemplation:
Upon a beam aloft he sits,
And nods, and seems to think, by fits.
So have I seen a man of news
Or Post-boy, or Gazette peruse,
Smoak, nod, and talk with voice profound,
And fix the fate of Europe round.
   Sheaves pil'd on sheaves hid all the floor:
At dawn of morn to view his store
The Farmer came. The hooting guest
His self-importance thus exprest.
   Reason in man is meer pretence:
How weak, how shallow is his sense!
To treat with scorn the bird of night,
Declares his folly or his spite;
Then too, how partial is his praise!
The lark's, the linnet's chirping lays
To his ill-judging ears are fine;
And nightingales are all divine.
But the more knowing feather'd race
See wisdom stampt upon my face.
Whene'er to visit light I deign,

What flocks of fowl compose my train!
Like slaves, they croud my flight behind,
And own me of superior kind.
   The Farmer laugh'd, and thus reply'd.
Thou dull important lump of pride,
Dar'st thou with that harsh grating tongue
Depreciate birds of warbling song?
Indulge thy spleen. Know, men and fowl
Regard thee, as thou art, an owl.
Besides, proud blockhead, be not vain
Of what thou call'st thy slaves and train.
Few follow wisdom or her rules,
Fools in derision follow fools.

TO THE OWL

By Thomas Russell

Grave Bird, that sheltered in thy lonely bower,
  On some tall oak with ivy overspread,
  Or in some silent barn's deserted shed,
  Or mid the fragments of some ruined tower,
Still, as of old, at this sad solemn hour,
  When now the toiling sons of care are fled,
  And the freed ghost slips from his wormy bed,
  Complainest loud of man's ungentle power,
That drives thee from the cheerful face of day
  To tell thy sorrows to the pale-eyed night,
  Like thee, escaping from the sunny ray,
I woo this gloom, to hide me from the sight
  Of that fell tribe, whose persecuting sway
  On me and thee alike is bent to light.

THE OWL

A FABLE

By Nathaniel Cotton

IT seems, an Owl, in days of yore,
Had turn'd a thousand volumes o'er:
His fame for literature extends,
And strikes the ears of partial friends.
They weigh'd the learning of the fowl,
And thought him a prodigious Owl!
From such applause what could betide?
It only cocker'd him in pride.
   Extoll'd for sciences and arts,
His bosom burn'd to show his parts;
(No wonder that an Owl of spirit
Mistook his vanity for merit.)
He shows insatiate thirst of praise,
Ambitious of the poet's bays:
Perch'd on Parnassus all night long,
He hoots a sonnet or a song;
And while the village hear his note,
They curse the screaming whoreson's throat.
   Amidst the darkness of the night,
Our feather'd poet wings his flight,
And, as capricious fate ordains,
A chimney's treacherous summit gains;
Which much impair'd by wind and weather,

Down fall the bricks and bird together.
   The Owl expands his azure eyes,
And sees a Non-con's study rise;
The walls were deck'd with hallow'd bands
Of worthies, by the' engraver's hands;
All champions for the good old cause!
Whose conscience interfer'd with laws;
But yet no foes to king or people,
Though mortal foes to church and steeple.
Baxter, with apostolic grace,
Display'd his mezzotinto face;
While here and there some luckier saint
Attain'd to dignity of paint.
   Rang'd in proportion to their size,
The books by due gradations rise.
Here the good Fathers lodg'd their trust;
There zealous Calvin slept in dust:
Here Poole his learned treasures keeps;
There Fox o'er dying martyrs weeps;
While reams on reams insatiate drink
Whole deluges of Henry's ink.
   Columns of sermons pil'd on high
Attract the bird's admiring eye.
Those works a good old age acquir'd,
Which had in manuscript expir'd;
For manuscripts, of fleeting date,
Seldom survive their infant state.
The healthiest live not half their days,
But die a thousand various ways;
Sometimes ingloriously applied
To purposes the Muse shall hide.
Or, should they meet no fate below,
How oft tobacco proves their foe!
Or else some cook purloins a leaf
To singe her fowl, or save her beef;

But sermons 'scape both fate and fire,
By congregational desire.
  Display'd at large upon the table
Was Bunyan's much-admired fable;
And as his Pilgrim sprawling lay,
It chanc'd the Owl advanc'd that way.
The bird explores the pious dream,
And plays a visionary scheme;
Determin'd, as he read the sage,
To copy from the tinker's page.
  The thief now quits his learn'd abode,
And scales aloft the sooty road;
Flies to Parnassus' top once more,
Resolv'd to dream as well as snore;
And what he dreamt by day, the wight
In writing o'er, consumes the night.
  Plum'd with conceit he calls aloud,
And thus bespeaks the purblind crowd;
Say not, that man alone's a poet,
Poets are Owls—my verse shall show it.
And while he read his labour'd lays,
His blue-eyed brothers hooted praise.
But now his female mate by turns
With pity and with choler burns;
When thus her consort she address'd,
And all her various thoughts express'd.
  'Why, prithee, husband, rant no more,
'Tis time to give these follies o'er.
Be wise, and follow my advice——
Go——catch your family some mice
'Twere better to resume your trade,
And spend your nights in ambuscade.
What! if you fatten by your schemes,
And fare luxuriously in dreams!
While you ideal mice are carving,

I and my family are starving.
Reflect upon our nuptial hours,
Where will you find a brood like our's?
Our offspring might become a queen,
For finer Owlets ne'er were seen!'
  "Ods—blue!' the surly hob reply'd,
'I'll amply for my heirs provide.
Why, Madge! when Colley Cibber dies,
Thou'lt see thy mate a laureate rise;
For never poets held this place,
Except descendants of our race.'
  'But soft,' the female sage rejoin'd—
'Say you abjur'd the purring kind;
And nobly left inglorious rats
To vulgar owls, or sordid cats.
Say, you the healing art essay'd,
And piddled in the doctor's trade;
At least you'd earn us good provisions,
And better this than scribbling visions.
A due regard to me, or self,
Would always make you dream of pelf;
And when you dreamt your nights away,
You'd realize your dreams by day.
Hence far superior gains would rise,
And I be fat, and you be wise.'
  'But, Madge, though I applaud your scheme,
You'd wish my patients still to dream!
Waking they'd laugh at my vocation,
Or disapprove my education;
And they detest your solemn hob,
Or take me for professor L——.'
  Equipt with powder and with pill,
He takes his licence out to kill.
Practis'd in all a doctor's airs,
To Batson's senate he repairs,

Dress'd in his flowing wig of knowledge,
To greet his brethren of the college;
Takes up the papers of the day,
Perhaps for want of what to say;
Through every column he pursues,
Alike advertisements and news;
O'er lists of cures with rapture runs,
Wrought by Apollo's natural sons;
Admires the rich Hibernian stock
Of doctors Henry, Ward, and Rock.
He dwells on each illustrious name,
And sighs at once for fees and fame.
Now, like the doctors of to-day,
Retains his puffers too in pay.
Around his reputation flew,
His practice with his credit grew.
At length the court receives the sage,
And lordlings in his cause engage.
He dupes, beside plebeian fowls,
The whole nobility of owls.
Thus every where he gains renown,
And fills his purse, and thins the town.

THE DICTATORIAL OWL

By Charlotte Smith

Within a hollow elm, whose scanty shade
But half acknowledg'd the returning spring,
A female Owl her domicile had made;
There, through the live-long day with folded wing
And eyes half-clos'd she sat; eyes black and round,
Like berries that on deadly nightshade grow,
And full white face demure, and look profound,
That ever seem'd some evil to foreknow;
Still with sententious saws she overflow'd,
And birds of omen dark frequented her abode.

Thither, to profit by her learned lore,
Repair'd the daw, the magpie, and the crow,
Malicious tongues indeed did say, that more
Of the vain world's affairs they wont to know,
And there discuss, than, 'mid the night's deep noon,
To hear wise axioms from her whisker'd beak,
Or to chaunt solemn airs to hail the moon;
But only worldlings thus, she said, would speak,
And, that more sapient judges did opine
Their converse was most pure, and held on themes divine.

She for the errours of the feather'd nation
Griev'd very sorely. "They were all infected
With vanities that wanted reformation,
And to erroneous notions were subjected;
Addicted too to sportiveness and joke,
To song and frolic, and profane delight;"
But Strixaline declar'd, the feather'd folk
Should be to grave demeanour given quite;
Nor, while rejoicing in the new-born spring,
Should cooing dove be heard, or woodlark carolling.

She often had to tell, in piteous tone,
How a poor chough by some sad chance was shent;
Or of some orphan cuckoo left alone
She would declaim; and then with loud lament,
To do them good, she'd their disasters tell,
And much deplore the faults they had committed;
Yet "hop'd, poor creatures! they might still do well."
And sighing, she would say, how much she pitied
Birds, who, improvident resolv'd to wed,
Which in such times as these to certain ruin led!

To her 'twas music, when grown gray with age,
Some crow caw'd loud her praise, with yellow bill,
And bade her in the wholesome task engage,
Mid the plum'd race new maxims to instill;
The raven, ever famous for discerning,
Of nose most exquisite for all good things,
Declar'd she was a fowl of wondrous learning;
And that no head was ever 'twixt two wings
So wise as hers. Nor female since the pope,
Ycleped Joan, with Strixaline could cope.

This, in process of time, so rais'd her pride,
That ev'ry hour seem'd lost, till she had shown
How science had to her no light denied,
And what prodigious wisdom was her own!
So, no more shrinking from the blaze of day.
Forth flew she. It was then those pleasant hours,
When village girls, to hail propitious May,
Search the wild copses and the fields for flow'rs,
And gayly sing the yellow meads among,
And ev'ry heart is cheer'd, and all look fresh and young.

His nest amid the orchard's painted buds
The bulfinch wove; and loudly sung the thrush
In the green hawthorn; and the new-leav'd woods,
The golden furze, and holly's guarded bush,
With song resounded: tree-moss gray enchas'd
The chaffinch's soft house; and the dark yew
Receiv'd the hedge sparrow, that careful plac'd
Within it's bosom eggs as brightly blue
As the calm sky, or the unruffled deep,
When not a cloud appears, and ev'n the zephyrs sleep.

There is a sundial near a garden fence,
Which flow'rs, and herbs, and blossom'd shrubs surround.
And Strixaline determin'd, that from thence
She to the winged creatures would expound
Her long collected store. There she alighted,
And, though much dazzled by the noon's bright rays,
In accents shrill a long discourse recited;
While all the birds, in wonder and amaze,
Their songs amid the coverts green suspended,
Much marvelling what Strixaline intended!

But when she told them, never joyous note
Should by light grateful hearts to Heav'n be sung,
And still insisted, that from ev'ry throat,
Dirges, the knell of cheerful Hope, be rung;
While, quitting meadows, wilds, and brakes, and trees,
She bade them among gloomy ruins hide;
Nor finch nor white-throat wanton on the breeze,
Nor reed lark warble by the river side;
They were indignant each, and stood aloof,
Suspecting all this zeal, but mask'd a shrewd Tartuffe.

Till out of patience they enrag'd surround her,
Some clamouring cry, that her insidious tongue
Bodes them no good; while others say they've found her
At ev'ning's close marauding for their young,
When frogs appear'd no more, and mice were scarce.
At length the wryneck, missel thrush, and bunting,
Protested they would end this odious farce,
And from the dial the baffl'd prater hunting,
With cries and shrieks her hooting they o'erwhelm,
And drive her back for shelter to her elm.

There, vanity severely mortified,
Still on her heart with sharp corrosion prey'd;
No salvo now could cure her wounded pride,
Yet did she fondly still herself persuade,
That she was born in a reforming hour,
And meant to dictate, govern, and direct;
That wisdom such as hers included pow'r,
Nor did experience teach her to reflect
How very ill *some folks* apply their labours,
Who think themselves much wiser than their neighbours.

OWL SONG

By Sir Walter Scott

"Of all the birds on bush or tree,
Commend me to the owl,
Since he may best ensample be
To those the cup that trowl.
For when the sun hath left the west,
He chooses the tree that he loves the best,
And he whoops out his song, and he laughs at his jest;
Then, though hours be late and weather foul,
We'll drink to the health of the bonny, bonny owl.

"The lark is but a bumpkin fowl,
He sleeps in his nest till morn;
But my blessing upon the jolly owl,
That all night blows his horn.
Then up with your cup till you stagger in speech,
And match me this catch till you swagger and screech,
And drink till you wink, my merry men each;
For, though hours be late and weather be foul,
We'll drink to the health of the bonny, bonny owl."

THE OWL

By Bryan Waller Procter

In the hollow tree, in the old gray tower,
   The spectral Owl doth dwell;
Dull, hated, despised, in the sunshine hour,
   But at dusk he's abroad and well!
Not a bird of the forest e'er mates with him;
   All mock him outright, by day;
But at night, when the woods grow still and dim,
   The boldest will shrink away!
      O, when the night falls, and roosts the fowl,
      Then, then, is the reign of the Hornéd Owl!

And the Owl hath a bride, who is fond and bold,
   And loveth the wood's deep gloom;
And, with eyes like the shine of the moonstone cold,
   She awaiteth her ghastly groom;
Not a feather she moves, not a carol she sings,
   As she waits in her tree so still;
But when her heart heareth his flapping wings,
   She hoots out her welcome shrill!
      O, when the moon shines, and dogs do howl,
      Then, then, is the joy of the Hornéd Owl!

Mourn not for the Owl, nor his gloomy plight!
  The Owl hath his share of good:
If a prisoner he be in the broad daylight,
  He is lord in the dark greenwood!
Nor lonely the bird, nor his ghastly mate,
  They are each unto each a pride;
Thrice fonder, perhaps, since a strange, dark fate
  Hath rent them from all beside!
    So, when the night falls, and dogs do howl,
    Sing, ho! for the reign of the Hornéd Owl!
      We know not alway
      Who are kings by day,
    But the King of the night is the bold brown Owl!

THE LEAVES
THAT RUSTLED ON THIS
OAK-CROWNED HILL

By William Wordsworth

The leaves that rustled on this oak-crowned hill,
And sky that danced among those leaves, are still;
Rest smooths the way for sleep; in field and bower
Soft shades and dews have shed their blended power
On drooping eyelid and the closing flower;
Sound is there none at which the faintest heart
Might leap, the weakest nerve of superstition start;
Save when the Owlet's unexpected scream
Pierces the ethereal vault; and ('mid the gleam
Of unsubstantial imagery, the dream,
From the hushed vale's realities, transferred
To the still lake) the imaginative Bird
Seems, 'mid inverted mountains, not unheard.

Grave Creature!—whether, while the moon shines bright
On thy wings opened wide for smoothest flight,
Thou art discovered in a roofless tower,
Rising from what may once have been a lady's bower;
Or spied where thou sitt'st moping in thy mew
At the dim centre of a churchyard yew;
Or, from a rifted crag or ivy tod
Deep in a forest, thy secure abode,
Thou giv'st, for pastime's sake, by shriek or shout,
A puzzling notice of thy whereabout—

May the night never come, nor day be seen,
When I shall scorn thy voice or mock thy mien!
In classic ages men perceived a soul
Of sapience in thy aspect, headless Owl!
Thee Athens reverenced in the studious grove;
And, near the golden sceptre grasped by Jove,
His Eagle's favourite perch, while round him sate
The Gods revolving the decrees of Fate,
Thou, too, wert present at Minerva's side:—
Hark to that second larum!—far and wide
The elements have heard, and rock and cave replied.

SONG — THE OWL

By Alfred Tennyson

I

WHEN cats run home and light is come,
  And dew is cold upon the ground,
And the far-off stream is dumb,
  And the whirring sail goes round,
  And the whirring sail goes round;
    Alone and warming his five wits,
    The white owl in the belfry sits.

II

When merry milkmaids click the latch,
  And rarely smells the new-mown hay,
And the cock hath sung beneath the thatch
  Twice or thrice his roundelay,
  Twice or thrice his roundelay;
    Alone and warming his five wits,
    The white owl in the belfry sits.

SECOND SONG

TO THE SAME

By Alfred Tennyson

I

THY tuwhits are lull'd, I wot,
  Thy tuwhoos of yesternight,
Which upon the dark afloat,
  So took echo with delight,
  So took echo with delight,
    That her voice, untuneful grown,
    Wears all day a fainter tone.

II

I would mock thy chaunt anew;
  But I cannot mimic it;
Not a whit of thy tuwhoo,
  Thee to woo to thy tuwhit,
  Thee to woo to thy tuwhit,
    With a lengthen'd loud halloo,
    Tuwhoo, tuwhit, tuwhit, tuwhoo-o-o!

THE OWL CRITIC

By James Thomas Fields

"WHO STUFFED that white owl?"
No one spoke in the shop;
The barber was busy, and he couldn't stop;
The customers, waiting their turns, were reading
The Daily, the Herald, the Post, little heeding
The young man who blurted out such a blunt question;
Not one raised a head, or even made a suggestion;
   And the barber kept on shaving.

"Don't you see, Mister Brown,"
Cried the youth with a frown,
"How wrong the whole thing is,
How preposterous each wing is,
How flattened the head, how jammed down the neck is —
In short, the whole owl, what an ignorant wreck 'tis!
"I make no apology;
I've learned owleology,
I've passed days and nights in a hundred collections,
And cannot be blinded to any deflections
Arising from unskilful fingers that fail
To stuff a bird right, from his beak to his tail.
Mister Brown, Mister Brown!
Do take that bird down,
Or you'll soon be the laughing stock all over town!"
   And the barber kept on shaving.

"I've *studied* owls,
And other night fowls,
And I tell you
What I know to be true!
An owl cannot roost
With his limbs so unloosed;
No owl in this world
Ever had his claws curled,
Ever had his legs slanted,
Ever had his bill canted,
Ever had his neck screwed
Into that attitude.
He can't *do* it, because
'Tis against all bird laws.
Anatomy teaches,
Ornithology preaches,
An owl has a toe
That *can't* turn out so!
I've made the white owl my study for years,
And to see such a job almost moves me to tears!
"Mister Brown, I'm amazed
You should be so crazed
As to put up a bird
In that posture absurd!
To *look* at that owl really brings on a dizziness;
The man who stuffed *him* don't half know his business!"
       And the barber kept on shaving.

"Examine those eyes,
I'm filled with surprise
Taxidermists should pass
Off on you such poor glass;
So unnatural they seem
They'd make Audubon scream,
And John Burroughs laugh
To encounter such chaff.
Do take that bird down;
Have him stuffed again, Brown!"
                    And the barber kept on shaving.

"With some sawdust and bark
I could stuff in the dark
An owl better than that.
I could make an old bat
Look more like an owl
Than that horrid fowl,
Stuck up there so stiff like a side of coarse leather;
In fact, about *him* there's not one natural feather."

Just then with a wink and a sly normal lurch,
The owl, very gravely, got down from his perch,
Walked round, and regarded his fault-finding critic,
(Who thought he was stuffed) with a glance analytic,
And then fairly hooted, as if he should say:
"Your learning's at fault, this time, anyway;
Don't waste it again on a live bird, I pray.
I'm an owl; you're another. Sir Critic, good-day!"
                    And the barber kept on shaving.

THE SULTAN
AND THE OWLS

AN ARABIAN TALE

By John Godfrey Saxe

I

THE Sultan, Mahmoud, in his early reign,
  By bootless foreign wars reduced the nation,
Till half his faithful followers were slain,
  And all the land was filled with desolation.

II

The Sultan's Vizier, saddened at the heart
  To see at every turn some new disaster,
Essayed in vain, by counsel and by art,
  To stay the folly of his royal master.

III

The Vizier, deeply versed in legal lore,
  In state affairs the Sultan's chief reliance,
Had found, besides, some leisure to explore
  In learned books the mysteries of science.

IV

With other matters of the graver sort,
   He knew to judge men's fancies by their features;
And understood, according to report,
   The hidden language of the feathered creatures.

V

One pleasant evening, on an aged tree,
   The while within a wood the twain were walking,
The Sultan and the Vizier chanced to see
   A pair of solemn owls engaged in talking.

VI

The Sultan asked: "What is it that they say?"
   And fain would know what the debate portended;
The Vizier answered: "Sire, excuse me, pray,
   I fear your Highness would be much offended."

VII

"Nay," said the Sultan, "whatsoe'er it be
   These heralds of Minerva may be saying,
Repeat it, Vizier, faithfully to me;
   There's no offence, except in not obeying."

VIII

"Well," said the other, "these sagacious fowls
   Have met, 't would seem, at the appointed hour,
To fix their children's wedding; and the owls
   Are at this moment talking of the dower.

IX

"The father of the daughter, speaking free,
   Says: 'What are your conditions? please to state 'em!'
   'Well, twenty ruined villages,' quoth he
(The father of the son); 'and that's my *ultimatum*!'

X

"'Done!' says the other, 'only understand
   I'd say two hundred quite as soon as twenty;
Thanks to good Mahmoud! while he rules the land
   We shall have ruined villages in plenty!'"

XI

'T is said the Sultan, stricken with remorse,
   Restored the land reduced by war and pillage,
And ruled so wisely in his future course
   That not an owl could find a ruined village.

THE EARLY OWL

By Oliver Herford

An owl once lived in a hollow tree,
And he was as wise as wise could be.
The branch of learning *he* didn't know
Could scarce on the tree of knowledge grow,
He knew the tree from branch to root,
And an owl like that can afford to hoot.

And he hooted—until, alas! one day,
　He chanced to hear, in a casual way,
An insignificant little bird
　Make use of a term he had never heard.
He was flying to bed in the dawning light
　When he heard her singing with all her might,
"Hurray! hurray! for the early worm!"

"Dear me," said the owl, "what a singular term!
I would look it up if it weren't so late,
　I must rise at *dusk* to investigate.
Early to bed and early to rise
　Makes an owl healthy, and stealthy, and wise!"

So he slept like an honest owl all day,
　And rose in the early twilight gray,
And went to work in the dusky light
　To look for the early worm at night.

He searched the country for miles around,
  But the early worm was not to be found;
So he went to bed in the dawning light
  And looked for the "worm" again next night.

And again and again, and again and again,
  He sought and he sought, but all in vain,
Till he must have looked for a year and a day
  For the early worm in the twilight gray.

At last in despair he gave up the search,
  And was heard to remark as he sat on his perch
By the side of his nest in the hollow tree:
  "The thing is as plain as night to me —
Nothing can shake my conviction firm.
  There's no such thing as the early worm."

THE PHILOSOPHER
AND THE OWL

By Jean Pierre Claris De Florian,
Translated by John Wolcott

Wrong'd, persecuted, and proscrib'd,
In foreign lands compell'd to hide,
For calling things by their right name,
A sage took with him all his wealth—
(His wisdom)—which he kept by stealth,
    And to a friendly forest came.
There, while pond'ring o'er his woes,
He saw an owl beset by foes—
An angry crowd of jays and crows.
They peck'd him, curs'd him, call'd him sot,
And said he was no patriot.
"Let's pluck him," said they, "of his plumes—
This rascal who such wit assumes!"
"Let's hang him," said the wrathful birds,
"And judge the villain afterwards!"

In vain the owl implor'd for peace,
And call'd on them their rage to cease.
The sage was touch'd to see the owl
Assail'd by words and deeds so foul
(For wisdom always makes the mind
To peace and gentleness inclin'd).
He quell'd the rage, and ask'd the bird
Why such a mob was 'gainst him stirr'd.
"Wherefore," said he, "is all this strife?
Why do these foes thus seek your life?"
"My only crime," the owl replied,
"Is one which they cannot abide;
The reason why I've rous'd their spite,
Is simply this—I see by night."

THE OWL AND THE CROW

By Benjamin Franklin King

THERE was an old owl,
　With eyes big and bright,
Who sung in a treetop
　One calm summer night.
And the song that he sung
　I will now sing to you —
"To whit! To whoo, hoo!
　To whit! To whoo, hoo!"

He sang there all night
　Till early next morn,
When a crow came along
　That was looking for corn.
The crow heard him singing,
　"To whit! To whoo, hoo!"
And offered to sing
　A few notes that he knew.

Just then the old owl
　In the treetop so high,
With his classical shape
　And his big staring eye,
Requested the crow,
　In the deepest of scorn,
To sing his old chestnut
　About stealing corn.

91

"Caw! Caw!" said the crow,
    "Well — my deeds are by light.
I don't steal young chickens
    And sit up all night,
With dew on my feathers;
    When I break the laws
In looking through cornfields
    It's not without caws"

OWL AGAINST ROBIN

By Sidney Lanier

FROWNING, the owl in the oak complained him
Sore, that the song of the robin restrained him
Wrongly of slumber, rudely of rest.
"From the north, from the east, from the south and the west,
Woodland, wheat-field, corn-field, clover,
Over and over and over and over,
Five o'clock, ten o'clock, twelve, or seven,
Nothing but robin-songs heard under heaven:
How can we sleep?

Peep! you whistle, and *cheep! cheep! cheep!*
Oh, peep, if you will, and buy, if 'tis cheap,
And have done; for an owl must sleep.
Are ye singing for fame, and who shall be first?
Each day's the same, yet the last is worst,
And the summer is cursed with the silly outburst
Of idiot red-breasts peeping and cheeping
By day, when all honest birds ought to be sleeping.
Lord, what a din! And so out of all reason.
Have ye not heard that each thing hath its season?
Night is to work in, night is for play-time;
Good heavens, not day-time!

A vulgar flaunt is the flaring day,
The impudent, hot, unsparing day,
That leaves not a stain nor a secret untold,—
Day the reporter,—the gossip of old,—
Deformity's tease, — man's common scold—
Poh! Shut the eyes, let the sense go numb
When day down the eastern way has come.
'Tis clear as the moon (by the argument drawn
From Design) that the world should retire at dawn.
Day kills. The leaf and the laborer breathe
Death in the sun, the cities seethe,
The mortal black marshes bubble with heat
And puff up pestilence; nothing is sweet
Has to do with the sun: even virtue will taint
(Philosophers say) and manhood grow faint
In the lands where the villainous sun has sway
Through the livelong drag of the dreadful day.
What Eden but noon-light stares it tame,
Shadowless, brazen, forsaken of shame?
For the sun tells lies on the landscape,—now
Reports me the *what*, unrelieved with the how,—
As messengers lie, with the facts alone,
Delivering the word and withholding the tone.

But oh, the sweetness, and oh, the light
Of the high-fastidious night!
Oh, to awake with the wise old stars—
The cultured, the careful, the Chesterfield stars,
That wink at the work-a-day fact of crime
And shine so rich through the ruins of time
That Baalbec is finer than London; oh,
To sit on the bough that zigzags low
        By the woodland pool,
And loudly laugh at man, the fool
That vows to the vulgar sun; oh, rare,

To wheel from the wood to the window where
A day-worn sleeper is dreaming of care,
And perch on the sill and straightly stare
Through his visions; rare, to sail
Aslant with the hill and a-curve with the vale,—

To flit down the shadow-shot-with-gleam,
Betwixt hanging leaves and starlit stream,
Hither, thither, to and fro,
Silent, aimless, dayless, slow
(*Aimless? Field-mice?* True, they're slain,
But the night-philosophy hoots at pain,
Grips, eats quick, and drops the bones
In the water beneath the bough, nor moans
At the death life feeds on.) Robin, pray
        Come away, come away
To the cultus of night. Abandon the day.
Have more to think and have less to say.
And *cannot* you walk now? Bah! don't hop!
        Stop!
Look at the owl, scarce seen, scarce heard,
O irritant, iterant, maddening bird!"

BALTIMORE, 1880.

95

Louis Agassiz Fuertes

TO A CAPTIVE OWL

By Henry Timrod

I should be dumb before thee, feathered sage!
   And gaze upon thy phiz with solemn awe,
But for a most audacious wish to gauge
   The hoarded wisdom of thy learned craw.

Art thou, grave bird! so wondrous wise indeed?
   Speak freely, without fear of jest or gibe—
What is thy moral and religious creed?
   And what the metaphysics of thy tribe?

A Poet, curious in birds and brutes,
   I do not question thee in idle play;
What is thy station? What are thy pursuits?
   Doubtless thou hast thy pleasures—what are *they?*

Or is't thy wont to muse and mouse at once,
   Entice thy prey with airs of meditation,
And with the unvarying habits of a dunce,
   To dine in solemn depths of contemplation?

There may be much—the world at least says so—
   Behind that ponderous brow and thoughtful gaze;
Yet such a great philosopher should know,
   It is by no means wise to think always.

And, Bird, despite thy meditative air,
   I hold thy stock of wit but paltry pelf—
Thou show'st that same grave aspect everywhere,
   And wouldst look thoughtful, stuffed, upon a shelf.

I grieve to be so plain, renowned Bird—
   Thy fame's a flam, and thou an empty fowl;
And what is more, upon a Poet's word
   I'd say as much, wert thou Minerva's owl.

So doff th' imposture of those heavy brows;
   They do not serve to hide thy instincts base—
And if thou must be sometimes munching *mouse,*
   Munch it, O Owl! with less profound a face.

THE ORACULAR OWL

By Amos Russel Wells

The oracular owl
Is a very wise fowl.
He sits on a limb
By night and by day.
And an eager assembly waits on him
To listen to what the wise bird may say.
I heard him discourse in the following way :
    "The sun soon will set in the west."
    Twill be fair if the sky is not cloudy."
    "If a hundred are good only one can be best."
    "No gentleman 's ever a rowdy."
"Ah I ah !" cry the birds. "What a marvellous fowl!
Oh, who could excel this oracular owl?"

THE OWL

By William Henry Davies

The boding Owl, that in despair
   Doth moan and shiver on warm nights—
Shall that bird prophesy for me
   The fall of Heaven's eternal lights?

When in the thistled field of Age
   I take my final walk on earth,
Still will I make that Owl's despair
   A thing to fill my heart with mirth.

DIRGE TO A DEAD OWL

By Patrick Reginald Chalmers

"Most proprietors nowadays strictly preserve these
beautiful and useful birds."

—*Natural History*

SILENT, mysterious, on wings of down,
A swift, deceptive presence in the cover,
Vaguely irresolute, soft-breasted, brown,
Bird of Minerva, tawny-eyed moon-lover,
You faced the sunshine mid the fir-trees gaunt,
Roused by the beaters' distant sticks a-tapping,
From some sequestered, hidden, noontide haunt,
Where doubtless you'd been napping.

Now all that's mortal of you, limp and dead,
Lies where a few pale, floating plumes still fly light;
Your little ghost, I like to think, has sped
To the dim nether world of endles twilight,
(Fit paradise for one who loved full well
The empty dark, those shores forlorn, abhorrent,)
To sail for ever o'er the asphodel
By Styx's gloomy torrent!

Meanwhile with hasty hands the mould I'll heap
Over your warm, uncaring, earthly habit,
Over the pinions that no more may sweep
Upon the unsophisticated rabbit;
Lost to the daylight (which you couldn't brook,
You loathed that sunrise bore, the dull but good cock),
None of the guns shall guess that I mistook
You for the sweepstakes woodcock.

THIS NIGHT

By William Henry Davies

This night, as I sit here alone,
And brood on what is dead and gone,
The owl that's in this Highgate Wood
Has found his fellow in my mood;
To every star, as it doth rise—
Oh-o-o! Oh-o-o! he shivering cries.

And, looking at the Moon this night,
There's that dark shadow in her light.
Ah! Life and Death, my fairest one,
Thy lover is a skeleton!
'And why is that?' I question—'why?'
Oh-o-o! oh-o-o! the owl doth cry.

THE OWL

By Philip Edward Thomas

Downhill I came, hungry, and yet not starved;
Cold, yet had heat within me that was proof
Against the North wind; tired, yet so that rest
Had seemed the sweetest thing under a roof.

Then at the inn I had food, fire, and rest,
Knowing how hungry, cold, and tired was I.
All of the night was quite barred out except
An owl's cry, a most melancholy cry

Shaken out long and clear upon the hill,
No merry note, nor cause of merriment,
But one telling me plain what I escaped
And others could not, that night, as in I went.

And salted was my food, and my repose,
Salted and sobered, too, by the bird's voice
Speaking for all who lay under the stars,
Soldiers and poor, unable to rejoice.

PROFUNDITY AND LEVITY

By Herman Melville

So frolic, so flighty,
Leaving wisdom behind,
Lark, little you ween
Of the progress of mind.
While fantastic you're winging,
Up-curving and singing,
A skylarking dot in the sun;
Under eaves here in wood
My wits am I giving
To this latest theme:
Life blinks at strong light,
Life wanders in night like a dream—
Is then life worth living?

BIBLIOGRAPHY

THE SEASONS—WHEN ICICLES HANG BY THE WALL
BY WILLIAM SHAKESPEARE,
   First published in *Love's Labour's Lost, Act* V, *Scene* 2, 1598
SWEET SUFFOLK OWL BY THOMAS VAUTOR,
   From *The First Set: Songs of Divers Airs and
   Natures,* 1619. A Musical Score.
THE TWO OWLS AND THE SPARROW BY JOHN GAY,
   First published under the title 'Fable XXXII. The Two
   Owls and the Sparrow' in *Fables, First Series,* 1727
THE OWL AND THE FARMER BY JOHN GAY,
   First published under the title 'Fable XLI. The Owl
   and the Farmer' in *Fables, First Series,* 1727
TO THE OWL BY THOMAS RUSSELL,
   First published under the title 'Sonnet XV. To the
   Owl' in *Sonnets and Miscellaneous Poems,* 1789
THE OWL—A FABLE BY NATHANIEL COTTON,
   From *Various Pieces in Verse and Prose,* 1791
THE DICTATORIAL OWL BY CHARLOTTE SMITH,
   First published posthumously in *A Natural History of Birds,
   Intended Chiefly for Young Persons, Volume* I of II, 1807
OWL SONG BY SIR WALTER SCOTT,
   First published in the novel, *Kenilworth,* 1821
THE OWL BY BRYAN WALLER PROCTER,
   First published under the title 'LXV. – The Owl' in
   English Songs: And Other Small Poems, 1832
THE LEAVES THAT RUSTLED ON THIS
OAK-CROWNED HILL BY WILLIAM WORDSWORTH,
   Written in 1834. First published in *Evening Voluntaries,* 1835

SONG—THE OWL BY ALFRED TENNYSON,
    First published in *Poems, Second Edition*, 1842
SECOND SONG—TO THE SAME BY ALFRED TENNYSON,
    First published in *Poems, Second Edition*, 1842
THE OWL CRITIC BY JAMES THOMAS FIELDS,
    First published in *Ballads and Other Verses*, 1881
THE SULTAN AND THE OWLS—AN ARABIAN TALE
BY JOHN GODFREY SAXE,
    First published in *The Poems of John Godfrey Saxe*, 1881
THE EARLY OWL BY OLIVER HERFORD,
    First published in *Artful Anticks*, 1888
THE PHILOSOPHER AND THE OWL
BY JEAN PIERRE CLARIS DE FLORIAN,
TRANSLATED BY JOHN WOLCOTT PHELPS,
    First published under the title 'Fable XXVII – The
    Philosopher and the Owl' in *The Fables of Florian,*
    Translated by John Wolcott Phelps, 1888
THE OWL AND THE CROW
BY BENJAMIN FRANKLIN KING JR.
    First published in *Ben King's Verse,* 1894
OWL AGAINST ROBIN BY SIDNEY LANIER,
    Published in *Poems of Sidney Lanierm,*
    Edited by his Wife, 1899
TO A CAPTIVE OWL BY HENRY TIMROD,
    First published posthumously in *Poems of Henry*
    Timrod; with Memoir by Henry Timrod, 1899
THE ORACULAR OWL BY AMOS RUSSEL WELLS,
    First published in *Rollicking Rhymes for Youngsters,* 1902
THE OWL BY WILLIAM HENRY DAVIES,
    First published in *Songs of Joy and Others,* 1911
DIRGE TO A DEAD OWL
BY PATRICK REGINALD CHALMERS,
    First published in *Green Days and Blue Days,* 1912
THIS NIGHT BY WILLIAM HENRY DAVIES,
    First published in *Child Lovers and Other Poems*, 1916

THE OWL BY PHILIP EDWARD THOMAS,
    First published in *Poems,* 1917
PROFUNDITY AND LEVITY BY HERMAN MELVILLE,
    First published in *Weeds and Wildings, With a Rose or
    Two,* 1924. A book of poems written for his wife and
    dedicated to her. Unpublished at the time of his death.

CPSIA information can be obtained
at www.ICGtesting.com
Printed in the USA
LVHW071347060322
712761LV00022B/1170

9 781528 719834